HARLEY-DAVIDSON

AMERICAN FREEDOM MACHINES

pil

Publications International, Ltd.

CREDITS

All photos by Doug Mitchel, except those from the Harley-Davidson Archives and Harley-Davidson Motor Company.

Front cover photography: Doug Mitchel
Additional art: Shutterstock.com

Preparing and completing a book of this magnitude requires the talents of many skilled individuals—including Tom Bolfert and Ray Schlee of the Harley-Davidson Archives. Their work however, would be impossible without the never-ending assistance of the owners of the great machines that fill these pages.

We would like to extend a very special thanks to the following owners and organizations:

John Archacki, Tom Baer, Rick Bernard, Marvin Bredemeir, Bud's Harley-Davidson, Don Chasteen, Al & Pat Doerman, David Freeman, Frank DeGenero, Henry Hack, Henry Hardin Family, Heritage Harley-Davidson, Illinois Harley-Davidson, Kersting's Harley-Davidson, Lake Shore Harley-Davidson, Greg Lew, Ted Moran, John Parham, Perfect Timing Inc., Elizabeth Phillips, Claudio Rauzi, Marty Rosenblum, Paul Ross, Steve Schifer, Robert Scott, Buzz Walneck, Walters Brothers Harley-Davidson, Stewart Ward, Wheels Through Time Museum

CONTENTS

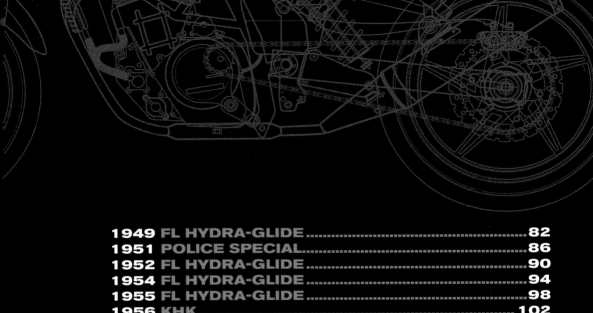

5

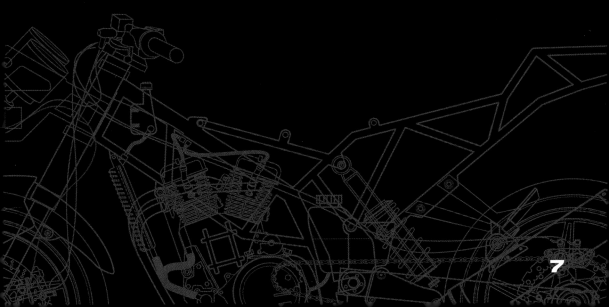

INTRODUCTION

Few could argue that Harley-Davidson is a name recognized—and revered—the world over. The company doesn't just produce motorcycles, it produces an American legend.

Not many businesses survive long enough to celebrate their 100th birthday, and fewer still manage to do so on the strength of their original product. Yet in 2003, Harley-Davidson celebrated 100 years of building just what it started out to make: distinctly American motorcycles. Today, Harley-Davidson looks to the future with plans to enter new market segments and even sell electric motorcycles.

THE EARLY YEARS

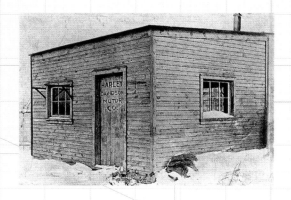

At the dawn of the 20th century, motorcycle production was already well underway in Europe but still in its infancy in the U.S. Yet by the time William Harley and brothers Arthur and Walter Davidson pieced together their first motorcycle in 1903, there were already a number of other domestic manufacturers, though most were little more than backyard enterprises. Among them was the Indian Motorcycle Company, founded in 1901, which would later become Harley's biggest competitor.

The first Harley-Davidson factory was a 10-foot by 15-foot structure located behind the Davidson's family home at 38th and Highland in Milwaukee. It was later expanded, but a larger building was constructed in 1907 at 38th and Chestnut, now known as Juneau—the site of the current headquarters. Shown on the opposite page in a circa 1910 photograph are the men whose names were on the building. Arthur Davidson, who recruited many dealers, Walter Davidson, who brought the company early competition success, William Harley, the engineer of the group, and William Davidson, oldest of the four.

The first Harley-Davidson differed little from other motorcycles of the time, essentially being a bicycle powered by a simple single-cylinder motor that drove the rear wheel through a leather belt. The normal pedals and chain remained in place so the rider could pedal the bike up to speed to start the motor, as well as lend a little leg power when ascending hills.

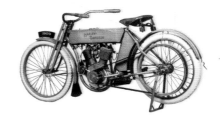

Though the 10.2 cubic-inch single-cylinder motor was patterned after an existing design, each part was made by hand. It managed to wheeze out only enough power to propel the machine to a brisk walking pace. A second example with a larger, more powerful motor followed, and it was this machine that formed the basis for the early production versions. Three motorcycles were built that year, and the Harley-Davidson Motor Company was in business.

Production rose to eight units in 1904, then to 16 the following year, reaching 50 in 1906, when the original black finish was joined by Renault Grey. In years to come, the company's quiet motors and grey paint would prompt riders to nickname Harleys the "silent grey fellows."

With the quest for more speed came the need for more power, and Harley-Davidson answered with its now-famous V-twin motor in 1909. The

first V-twin proved trouble-prone and was discontinued. Harley didn't give up. An improved V-twin returned for 1911 and a legend was born.

With that Harley-Davidson's technology began advancing at a rapid rate. The company introduced one of the industry's first clutches in 1912, chain drive became available in 1913, and a two-speed rear hub debuted for 1914, followed by a proper three-speed sliding-gear transmission the next year.

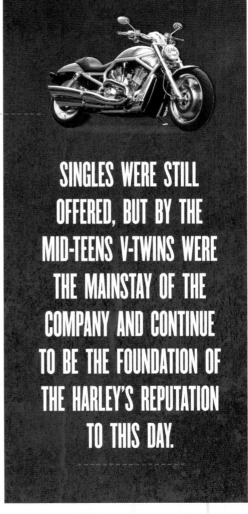

SINGLES WERE STILL OFFERED, BUT BY THE MID-TEENS V-TWINS WERE THE MAINSTAY OF THE COMPANY AND CONTINUE TO BE THE FOUNDATION OF THE HARLEY'S REPUTATION TO THIS DAY.

1903 HD

THE FIRST MOTORCYCLE BUILT BY WILLIAM HARLEY AND BROTHERS ARTHUR AND WALTER DAVIDSON TOOK SHAPE IN 1903.

1903 HD | 15

Power came from a hand-made 10.2-cubic-inch motor based on a DeDion (of France) design, with a vacuum-activated overhead intake valve and a mechanically operated side exhaust valve. Afterward came a stronger machine with a loop-style frame and more powerful 25-cubic-inch motor, and this was the form taken by the first production models in 1903.

FEATURED IS HARLEY-DAVIDSON SERIAL NUMBER ONE THAT CURRENTLY RESIDES IN A GLASS CASE IN THE RECEPTION AREA OF THE JUNEAU AVENUE HEADQUARTERS.

1905

HD

Two years after the first Harley-Davidson had chugged its way along the streets of Milwaukee, the motorcycles had changed little in appearance.

Power from the 24.74-cubic-inch motor was enough to propel the machine to a reported 25 mph or so.

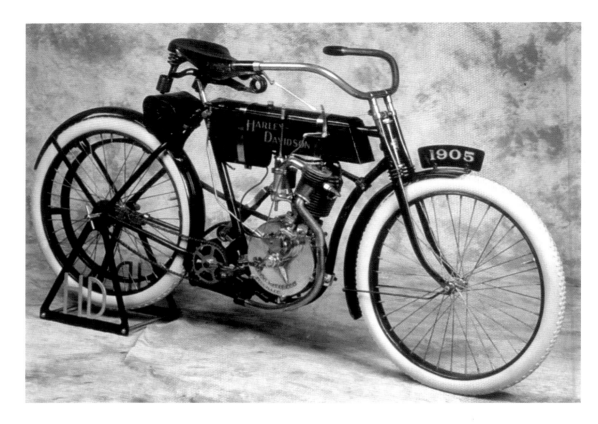

By that time, their numbers had also increased dramatically: Eight of the shiny black machines had been built during 1904, with another sixteen hitting the streets in 1905.

The tall lever along the left side of the fuel tank adjusted tension on the leather drive belt. Since modern control cables had not yet been invented, intricate jointed shafts were used for

throttle and other controls. The motor still used a vacuum-operated over-head intake valve and mechanically actuated side exhaust valve. A trio of batteries supplied juice to the ignition, but there was no on-board method for recharging it. To start the motor, riders would pedal the motorcycle up to speed—not an easy task, as they were not only propelling a heavy bike, but also turning over the motor.

1909

V-TWIN

Harley's first production V-twin arrived in 1909. By this time, grey had replaced black as the standard color, and Sager-Cushion front forks were used that allowed a small amount of front wheel travel.

Cylinders were the same size as those used for the single, displacement coming out to 49.48 cubic inches. The "V" measured 45 degrees—as have all street Harley V-twins until the 2002 V-Rod.

THE HARLEY-DAVISON FACTORY AS IT APPEARED IN 1908. THE BUILDING HAD BEEN CONSTRUCTED TWO YEARS EARLIER ON A NEW SITE AT 38TH AND CHESTNUT (NOW JUNEAU)

That first V-twin didn't fare well, however, one problem being that the vacuum-operated intake valves did not function correctly. The V-twin was withdrawn from the market for a year, and when it returned for 1911, it had mechanical intake valves. The following year, displacement was increased to 61 cubic inches.

1912

X8A

Though the V-twins that made Harley-Davidson famous appeared in 1909, single-cylinder machines continued to represent the bulk of Harley's sales. By 1912, public demand for more power was answered with the X8A, which was powered by a 30-cubic-inch single producing 4.3 horsepower.

A hand-operated oil pump was added to augment the existing gravity-feed system, and a magneto ignition was used for easier starting. Also new this year was the "Free Wheel Control," one of the industry's first clutch systems. With it, smooth takeoffs from a standing start were possible for the first time.

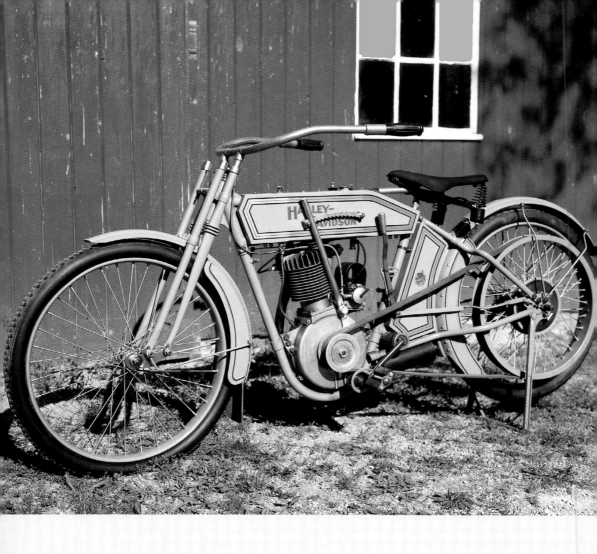

The issue of comfort was also addressed. Joining Harley's traditional leading-link front fork was the new "Full Floating" saddle, in which a coil spring mounted inside the vertical frame tube cushioned the seat post, while the rear of the seat was supported by two more coils. Though this was hardly a substitute for a real rear suspension, it was as good as Harley riders would get for another 45 years.

1915

11-F

AFTER THE SUCCESSFUL RELAUNCH OF THE V-TWIN IN 1911, TECHNOLOGY PROGRESSED AT A RAPID RATE.

Chain final drive replaced the slip-prone belt for 1913, and the following year brought floorboards, a forward-stroke kick starter (using the supplied bicycle pedals), enclosed exhaust-valve springs, and a two-speed rear hub.

A three-speed transmission and electric lighting were made available for 1915, though this example carries an "old fashioned" acetylene-powered headlight.

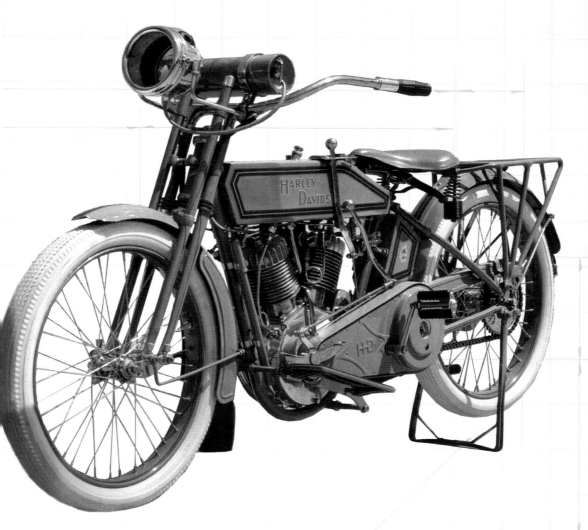

1915 11-F | 31

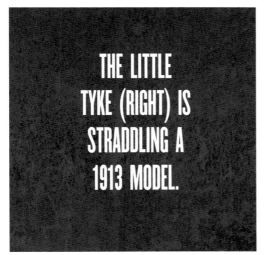

THE LITTLE TYKE (RIGHT) IS STRADDLING A 1913 MODEL.

1916

16-J

New styling graced the 1916 Harleys, the most notable element being a sleeker fuel tank with rounded contours. Also new was a modern rear-stroke kick lever that finally did away with the bicycle-style pedals fitted to earlier models. These two changes may seem minor in today's light, but were notable steps in the move from motorized bicycles to true motorcycles.

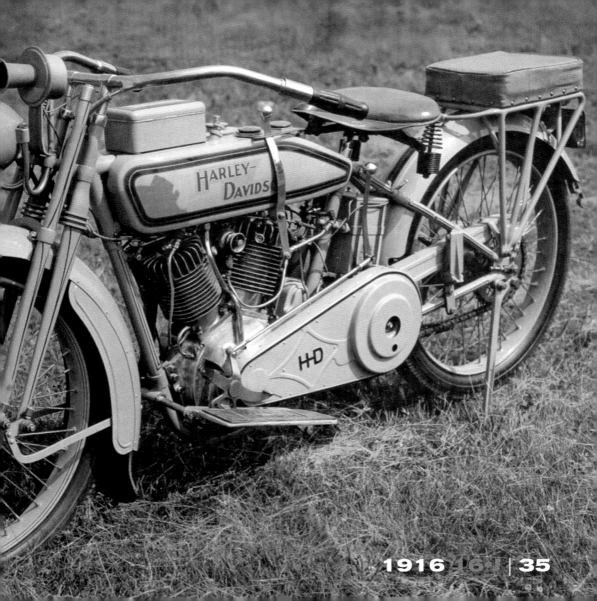

Previously, model designations started with the number of years after 1904 that the machine was built. In 1916, the actual model year was used instead, with the following letter an indication of such features as a generator (J) or magneto (F).

1918

18-J

The Model J was Harley's most powerful motorcycle for 1918. As such, it was well suited for use with the matching sidecar, which afforded its occupants far more luxury—and better weather protection—than the motorcycle's rider enjoyed. Though electric lighting was available, this example is fitted with an acetylene-powered headlight and taillights that were fed from a tank mounted on the handle bars.

1918 18-J | **39**

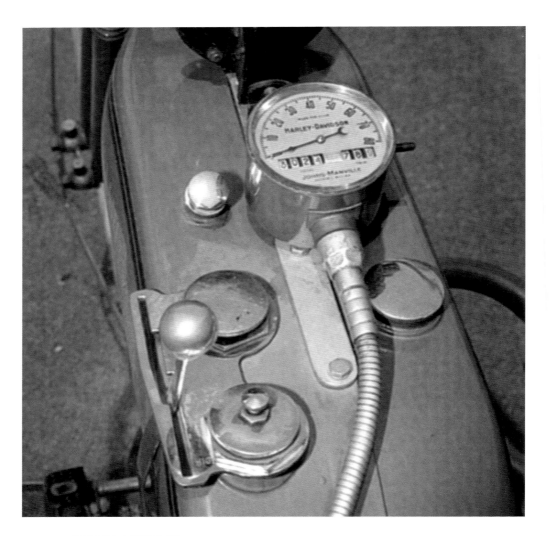

As it had since 1915, the tank-mounted speedometer was driven by a gear on the rear wheel. The staggered shifter gate for the three-speed transmission placed first gear toward the front, with neutral, second, and third to the rear.

1920

20-J

Harley-Davidson switched to olive paint for its 1917 models. Styling changes were few during those years, the most notable occurring in 1920 when the headlight and horn switched places. V-twins still displaced the same 61 cubic inches (1000-cc) as before, though a 74-cubic-inch (1200-cc) model joined the line for 1921.

During the early Twenties, Harley-Davdison sponsored an extremely successful racing team, which became know as the wrecking crew for the way it demolished its opponents. Racing models were devoid of such luxuries as sprung seats and even brakes, and some boasted special overhead-valve engines with two or four valves per cylinder. The 1922 JD racer (shown above) is fitted with Harley's conventional F-head (overhead intake valve and side exhaust valve) engine, and like Harley competition bikes of the era, carries bolder tank lettering for promotional purposes.

1925

JD

Brewster Green replaced olive in 1922, and 1923 models ushered in a hinged rear fender that simplified tire changes. Oddly, olive returned as the standard color in '24, when a box-shaped muffler was fitted for that year only.

1925 JD | **47**

A redesign for 1925 brought a huskier look with a lower frame, more streamlined fuel tank, and smaller-diameter but beefier tires. Seat height dropped by three inches, and the seat itself was "bucket-type" rather than the flat bicycle-style used previously. Mufflers reverted to tubular shape. Optional colors became available in 1926 (though they weren't mentioned in any sales literature), and Harley's famous "waste spark" distributorless ignition system debuted for 1927.

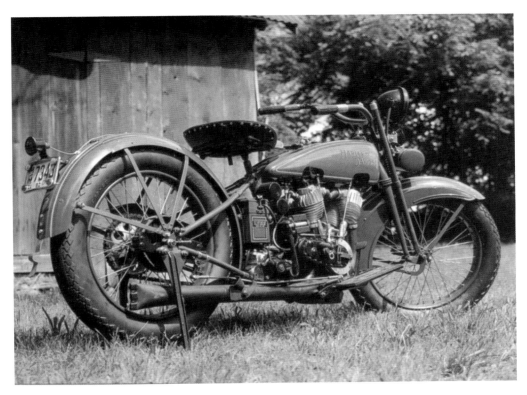

Front brakes appeared for 1928, as did high performance Two Cam variants of the 61- and 74-cubic-inch V-twins (called JH and JDH, respectively). These were among the fastest bikes of the day, capable of hitting 85 mph off the showroom floor. But by this time, F-head engineering had advanced about as far as it could go, and its days were numbered.

1927
BA

Though economical to buy and run, Harley's 21-cubic-inch single never sold particularly well during its ten-year production run. However, competition versions, known as "peashooters" due to the sound of their exhaust note, claimed many victories at the hands of Joe Petrali during the same period.

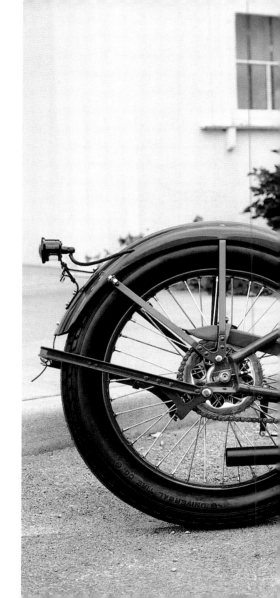

1927 **BA** | 51

Two versions of the single were offered: a "Flathead" with eight horsepower and an overhead-valve variant producing twelve horsepower—an impressive 50 percent increase.

Yet the "Flathead" sold better due to its lower cost and easier maintenance. Both could be fitted with electric lighting like the "Flathead" shown.

Learn to Ride it in the Length of a City Block

HARLEY-DAVIDSON
"Single"

DOWN goes your foot on the kick starter, and the motor starts. Step on the clutch. Slip the gearshift into low. Now you're riding.

Learn? Nothing to it! In the length of a city block you can learn to ride the New Harley-Davidson Single. Why, it's far easier to learn to ride than a bicycle—no pedaling. Once under way, this New Single almost keeps its own balance.

Here is a new type motorcycle that is safe and simple to operate—that is easy to ride and handle. It is low in first cost and cheap to upkeep. Think of it—80 miles and more to a gallon of gas, 800 miles to a gallon of oil, 10,000 to 12,000 miles to a set of two inexpensive tires. Forget about big garage expense—takes little more space than a bicycle!

With this new Single you can ride right up where you want to go—pack it anywhere. It will take you wherever you want to go—and has all the power and speed you need. It is just the motorcycle you have often thought about and wanted—a single cylinder, easy and safe to ride, low in price, cheap in upkeep. Drop over to the Harley-Davidson dealer and see it.

HARLEY-DAVIDSON MOTOR COMPANY, MILWAUKEE, WIS.

America's preference for big, powerful twins led to the demise of these single-cylinder models in the 1930s. Harley continued for a time with a larger 30.5-cubic-inch single and made several later attempts at selling single-cylinder machines, but it was always V-twins for which the company was best known.

1931

MODEL D

...arley began switching from F-head to ...thead (side valve) V-twins in 1929. First ...me a new 45-cubic-inch model intended ...compete with Indians' highly successful ...out. The following year, the 61- and ...-cubic-inch Big Twins were changed ...er to a flathead design.

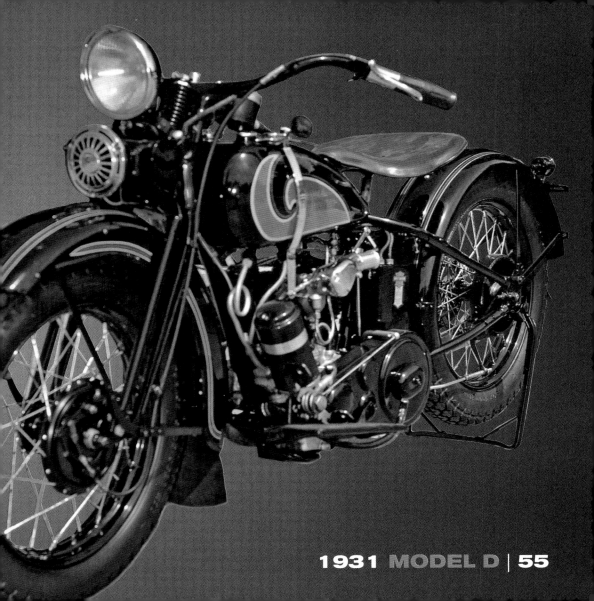

1931 MODEL D | 55

This 1931 Model D is a 45-cid version. Forty-fives look very similar to their bigger brothers and oftentimes the easiest way to tell them apart is that the Forty-fives drive chain is on the right instead of the left.

Prior to 1933, Harley-Davidson offered custom paint jobs that could be ordered in place of the standard olive. In 1933, the standard finish switched to a choice of two-tone colors with "eagle motif" graphics (above), though olive was still available.

1934

VLD

Color choices widened as Harley-Davidson battled the effects of the Depression. The Seventy-four shown here sports a black with Orlando Orange paint scheme that was a no-charge option. It's also fitted with an optional Buddy Seat, a two-passenger saddle that debuted in 1933 and proved very popular.

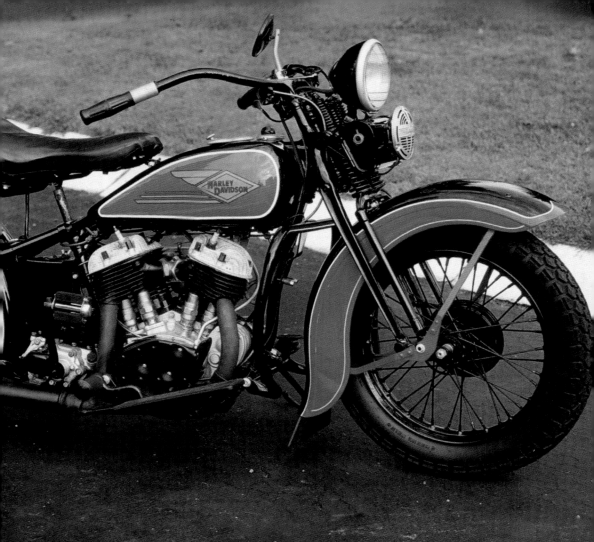

Instead of the colorful two-tone paint schemes offered in 1934, this 74-cubic-inch VLD—along with its matching sidecar—is painted in the old Olive hue. Styling revisions for 1934 included new streamlined fenders. A small windshield mounted on a protective tonneau shielded the sidecar passenger. The tonneau and windshield could fold forward to ease entry/exit.

Harleys used a hand shift/foot clutch arrangement until 1952, and continued to offer it as an option into the Seventies. On early Harleys, the clutch was engaged by pushing down with the toes, and disengaged by pushing down with the heel.

1936

EL

With speed becoming a greater priority to many riders, Harley introduced the 61 OHV in 1936. The new 61-cubic-inch V-twin boasted overhead valves, and was soon christened the "Knucklehead" by owners due to its valve cover design, which looked like a fist with two knuckles sticking out.

Though the knucklehead spotted nearly 20 cubic inches to its biggest flathead sibling, it produced more power, and would be the basis for all big twin engines for the next sixty-some years.

The knucklehead powered model was given the E-Series designation, and carried another element of historical significance: Harley's first tank-mounted instrument panel. Two-tone paint schemes for 1936 ranged from mild (black and red) to wild (maroon and Nile Green, as shown above left, on a 74-cubic-inch flathead).

1938

UL

DESPITE THE POPULARITY OF THE KNUCKLEHEAD, HARLEY CONTINUED TO OFFER FLATHEAD BIG TWINS.

1938 **UL** | 67

An 80-cubic-inch flathead joined
the existing 74 late in the 1935 model
year, and for 1937, both gained the
recirculating oiling system introduced
on the Knucklehead. (Previously a

"total loss" lubrication system was
used.) The bikes they powered also
adopted the Knucklehead's styling,
and these changes prompted new
model designations: U for the Seven-

ty-four, UH for the Eighty. High-compression versions of both carried an L as the second letter, so this UL is a high-compression Seventy-four. The Eighty was dropped shortly after the introduction of a 74-cubic-inch Knucklehead in 1941, but the Seventy-four flathead would carry on through 1948.

1942
WLA

THOUGH RIVAL INDIAN ALSO SUPPLIED
MOTORCYCLES TO THE U.S. MILITARY DURING
WORLD WAR II, THE MAJORITY OF THOSE USED
IN BATTLE WERE HARLEY-DAVIDSON WLAs.

Wearing the requisite Olive Drab paint, these were 45-cubic-inch V-twin flatheads fitted with special equipment for wartime use. Items such as an ammo box, machine-gun scabbard, and rear carrier are obvious. In all, roughly 80,000 WLAs were built, many being sold as surplus after the war—some for as little as $25.

These surplus WLAs were often stripped down and fitted with aftermarket parts, fueling the rapidly developing customizing trend.

1947 SERVI-CAR

When introduced for the 1933 model year, the three-wheeled Servi-Car was intended for use by auto repair shops to make house calls. If the mechanic couldn't make the necessary repairs with the tools stored in the cargo box, he could hitch his mount to the rear bumper of the car with a tow bar, and (assuming the car was drive-able), take the two of them back to the garage. Likewise, it could also be used to deliver the car when the work was completed.

1947 SERVI-CAR | 75

Over the years, Servi-Cars have been used for all sorts of chores, one of the more common being for parking enforcement. Our featured example was purchased by the Milwaukee Police Department for just that purpose. Note the chalk stick attached to the box behind the seat. Since cars were parked on the right (and therefore the officer would be wielding the stick in his right hand), the throttle is on the left. That necessitated moving the shifter to the right, so this vehicle is set up just the opposite of most.

Servi-Cars were powered by the 45-cubic-inch flathead V-twin and normally fitted with a three-speed transmission with reverse. The '64 model was the first Harley with electric starting. They remained in production through 1973, carrying the old 45 fathead to the end.

1947 SERVI-CAR | 77

1948

WL

Harley-Davidson's first "flathead" V-twin appeared in 1929 as the Model D. Its 45-cubic-inch engine was smaller than the company's existing 61- and 74-cubic-inch "F-head" V-twins, which then became known as "Big Twins." The latter switched to a flathead design the following year, but those larger engines were neither as reliable nor as long-lived as the under-stressed Forty-five.

Though the Forty-five was no pow-
erhouse, it proved to be a versatile
engine that remained in production
for more than four decades. During
that time it served duty not only in
street motorcycles, but also
in three-wheeled Servi-Cars
(1933-1973), military WLAs of the
1940s, and WR racing bikes of the
1940s and 1950s.

By 1948, the Forty-five was powering a street model called the WL. It looked very similar to Harley's Big Twin flatheads of the era, the most noticeable visual difference being that WLs had their drive chains on the right side of the bike, while Big Twins had them on the left. Though 1948 would prove to be the final year for Big Twin flatheads, the WL lasted through 1951, after which it was replaced by the K-series carrying a redesigned 45-cubic-inch flathead V-twin with unit construction (motor and transmission in one case).

1949

FL HYDRA-GLIDE

While the Panhead engine of 1948, with its overhead valves and aluminum head, was heralded as a major advancement, perhaps even more newsworthy was the introduction of "Hydra-Glide" front forks the following year. Replacing the leading-link springer front ends, these modern hydraulic forks afforded better ride control while providing twice the wheel travel.

So revolutionary were these new forks—at least for Harley—that the motorcycle itself was named after them, EL (61 cubic inch) and FL (74 cubic inch) designation remained, and initial ads referred only to "the Hydra-Glide fork," but later models had "Hydra-Glide" stamped into the headlight backing plate and (in '57) emblazoned on the front fender.

1951
POLICE SPECIAL

Harley's police motorcycles not only came with a wide assortment of equipment specific to their duties, but were often available in colors not offered on civilian bikes.

Before the war they were usually painted Police Blue, but many post-war models came in Police Silver. Restoration of a police bike is more difficult due to the added equipment, which itself needs to be restored as reproductions are hard to find. The left-side "saddlebag" is actually a two-way radio; a brass fire extinguisher resides on the right.

Not all police bikes were dressed in such a bright uniform. Many were almost devoid of chrome trim, having fork legs, wheels, and primary cases painted black. Harley's first police bike was put in use by the city of Detroit, Michigan, in 1908.

1952

FL HYDRA-GLIDE

The next major advancement for Big Twins came in 1952, when the old hand-shift/foot-clutch arrangement was superseded by a modern foot shift and hand clutch. However, the old setup was still optionally available—and would remain so until the mid-Seventies—as it was still preferred by some riders and police departments.

1952 FL HYDRA-GLIDE | 91

Never one to turn a deaf ear to its customer's wishes, Harley continued to lavish its bikes with more chrome and polished pieces. Some additional brightwork was made standard, such as polished lower fork legs (which were at first painted black), while accessory packages offered such niceties as chrome fender rails, chrome instrument panel, and chrome front-fender lamp. Also, the 61-cubic-inch (EL) version of the Panhead was dropped after 1952 due to lack of interest, leaving the 74-cid FL as the only Big Twin.

On the flathead front, the faithful 45-cubic-inch WL was superseded

by the Model K, which was entirely redesigned. New features included a foot-shift transmission in unit with a reworked 45-inch flathead V-twin, hydraulic front forks (the WL kept its old springer till the end), and Harley's first rear suspension, a conventional swingarm with dual coil-over shocks.

1952 FL HYDRA-GLIDE | 93

1954

FL HYDRA-GLIDE

A special "50 Years" badge graced Harley-Davidson's 1954 V-twins, because 1904 was considered the start of actual production. However, some 1903 Harleys *were* sold (even though they weren't considered true production models), and it was later decided that subsequent anniversary celebrations would reflect the company's 1903 founding.

Color-matched hand grips and kick-lever pedal were popular dealer accessories of the period. The model above wears two-tone paint (tank and fenders in contrasting colors) and dual exhausts, both of which were factory options.

1955

FL HYDRA-GLIDE

New Big Twin features for 1955 included revised cast tank badges boasting a prominent "V" in the background, along with a similar badge on the front fender with "1955" stamped into it. Meanwhile, taillights switched from the old "tombstone" style (which had been in use for nearly a decade) to a new oval design. Also, the existing FL was joined by a performance-oriented FLH with higher

compression, hotter cams, and polished ports that resulted in about 10 percent more power. Standard equipment included a Jubilee air trumpet, and a host of optional accessories were available; those fitted to our featured model include body-colored hand grips, chrome luggage rack, chrome engine guard, Buddy Seat with chrome grab rail, chrome fender dressing, and other chrome touches. By this time, chrome trim had become a popular means of dressing up and personalizing one's mount.

1956
KHK

WHEN IT REPLACED THE W-SERIES IN 1952, THE ALL-NEW K-SERIES MAINTAINED THE 45-CUBIC-INCH ENGINE DISPLACEMENT AND SIDE VALVES OF ITS PREDECESSOR.

For 1954, however, the engine was enlarged to 55 cubic inches and the model designation changed to KH.

In either case, a "K" suffix indicated a sport model with lower handlebars, less chrome trim, and performance-oriented cams.

The KH evolved into the overhead-valve Sportster in 1957, so this 1956 KHK represents the last of its breed—and the last flathead V-twin motorcycle (save for the three-wheel Servi-Car) Harley-Davidson would ever offer.

1957

XL SPORTSTER

After World War II, sporting British middleweights began attracting a growing number of enthusiasts in the U.S.

Despite larger displacements, Harley's K and KH flatheads had a hard time keeping up with the more advanced overhead-valve offerings from England, so the company's midsized V-twin was itself converted to overhead valves for 1957. This resulted in the famed 883-cc (55 cubic inch) XL Sportster, which would rule dragstrips for the next decade.

Like the K-Series that preceded it, the Sportster's transmission was in unit with the engine. (By contrast, Big Twins had separate engines and transmissions.) The chassis was carried over virtually unchanged, though a new badge, which was used on all Harley V-twins that year, graced the fuel tank.

1958

FL DUO-GLIDE

After more than 50 years of hardtail riding, Harley-Davidson treated Big Twin buyers to "The Glide Ride" for 1958. With a conventional swing arm suspension added to the rear, the Hydra-Glide became the Duo-Glide, a transition evidenced not only by the large chrome-covered shocks in back, but also by prominent lettering on the fender in front.

Our featured example is fitted with a host of popular contemporary accessories, including auxiliary driving lights, windshield, engine guard, Buddy Seat with passenger grab bar, luggage rack, saddle bags, and turn signals, items that transformed it into what is popularly known as a "dresser."

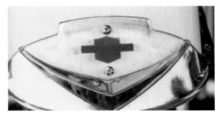

1959
POLICE SPECIAL

HARLEY'S BIG TWINS HAVE ALWAYS BEEN POPULAR WITH MUNICIPALITIES, MOST BEING USED FOR POLICE DUTY.

This example, however, was pressed into duty as a funeral escort.

Though it missed out on all the excitement enjoyed by its police-ridden siblings, it has nothing to be ashamed of, as it carries many of the same accessories—siren, red lights, and radio—as the pursuit models. It also wears the special silver paint that was reserved for police bikes, and unlike the civilian models, is not two-toned.

Though a hand-clutch /foot-shift arrangement had been standard since 1952, many police departments opted for the old hand shifter. That way, the foot clutch could be disengaged, allowing the bike to be left in gear with the motor running.

1959

XLCH SPORTSTER

A hotter version of the Sportster was introduced in 1958 under the XLCH tag. Intended as a performance-oriented on/off road machine (rumor had it the "C" stood for "Competition," though Harley never said one way or the other), the 1959 XLCH differed from its milder XLH sibling by sporting magneto ignition, high-mounted exhaust pipe, "peanut" fuel tank, "bobbed" rear fender, and semi knobby tires.

Tank badges were also different, being of a design shared by some of Harley's contemporary racing bikes. The "H" on the decal stood for "Hot". The XLCH also debuted the "eyebrow" headlight cover that

remained a Sportster trademark for many years.

By contrast, the touring-oriented XLH looked (and was) heavier, with fuller fenders, large headlight nacelle, larger fuel and oil tanks, and low exhaust. Harley-Davidson maintained these two Sportster models through 1979, during which time they proved very successful, both on the racetrack and in the showroom.

1963

FL DUO-GLIDE

ASIDE FROM A NEW TANK BADGE AND PAINT SCHEME, THE FL DIDN'T CHANGE MUCH FOR '63.

However, Harley had tried something different for the '61 models, when the age-old "waste spark" ignition was traded for a more modern—but more complicated —system employing two sets of points and coils.

The experiment only lasted through 1964, after which the waste-spark setup returned.

This is a fairly stripped example of the big FL, as most were fitted with saddlebags and two-passenger

Buddy Seat—in addition to the windshield—all being requisites for the well-dressed touring motorcycle.

1965

FL ELECTRA-GLIDE

FOR THE FIRST TIME SINCE 1958, THE FL WAS TREATED TO SOMETHING REALLY NEW: AN ELECTRIC STARTER.

No longer did Harley riders have to struggle to kick over the big 74-cubic-inch V-twin—which had a nasty habit of kicking back. Some riders shunned the idea of an "electric leg," but it was the final step in making the newly named Electra-Glide a true luxury tourer.

Along with the electric starter came a commensurately larger battery, both of which added more weight to a bike that was decidedly plump to begin with. As a result, fully optioned Electra-Glides could now tip the scales at over 800 pounds.

1966
FL
ELECTRA-GLIDE

With increased weight came decreased performance, so it was decided the venerable Panhead, which had served faithfully for 18 years, was due for a freshening. The replacement arrived for 1966, and would itself enjoy a lengthy tenure between the frame rails of Harley's biggest bikes.

Like its predecessors, the new engine was quickly given a nickname based on the shape of its valve covers, which now resembled inverted shovel scoops. Horsepower of the "Shovelhead" rose by less than 10 percent (from an advertised 60 to 65), but with this much mass to move, every little bit helped.

1967

XLH SPORTSTER

FOR 1967, SPORTSTERS OFFERED THE ELECTRIC STARTER INTRODUCED ON BIG TWINS TWO YEARS EARLIER.

1967 XLH SPORTSTER | 135

However, it was only available on the "luxury" XLH version; the sportier XLCH stuck with a kick starter, which remained on the XLH as a back-up to the electric leg.

As before, the XLH also carried fancier trim, including a large polished headlight nacelle, chromed rear shock covers, and a larger fuel tank.

Harley-Davidson ads in 1967 boasted of the
Sportster's record-setting runs at Bonneville.
Though these were highly modified machines,
the company could still claim that "nobody
builds a faster stock motorcycle."

1971

FX SUPER GLIDE

At a time when many bikes fell victim to the customizer's torch just miles out of the showroom, Harley decided to save people the trouble by creating a custom of its own. The design has been credited to Willie G. Davidson, grandson of one of the founders, who was employed in a styling department that was now under the watchful eye of the company's AMF parent.

Combining the 1200-cc FL engine and frame with the lighter XL (Sportster) front end prompted the FX-1200 designation. In addition, a special stepped seat and "boat-tail" rear fender (patterned after the one used on the previous year's Sportster) were fitted, and the end result was christened the Super Glide.

Early models came only with a kick starter, but an electric starter was offered for 1974, by which time the bike also had a front disc brake.

Though it's a coveted collectible today, the original Super Glide didn't go over all that well. But it introduced the idea of the factory custom, which over the years has been a strong and profitable market segment for Harley-Davidson.

1971

XLH SPORTSTER

The boat-tail rear fender design that graced the Super Glide for 1971 originated on the 1970 Sportster. It didn't enjoy universal appeal, but it was offered again for '71 Sportsters as a $60 option. Also optional was the red, white, and blue Sparkling America paint scheme, along with colors such as the Sparkling Turquoise worn by this example. None proved popular enough to warrant a return engagement for '72.

Sportster engines still displaced 883-cc in 1971; for '72, that would be boosted to 1000-cc, a move prompted by the growing number of large-displacement Japanese bikes that were beginning to crowd Harley out of the big-bore sport market.

1971 XLH SPORTSTER | 145

1973
FL ELECTRA-GLIDE

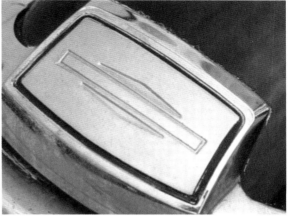

THOUGH PURCHASED BY AMF IN JANUARY OF 1969, "AMF" DIDN'T BEGIN TO APPEAR ON HARLEY BADGING UNTIL 1971.

When it did, many owners—not altogether happy about the association—removed the badges and repainted the bike. As a result, relatively few Harleys from the AMF years survive in unmolested condition.

This one did, however. It isn't in pristine shape because it's never even been restored. Save for the inevitable ravages of Father Time, it's an original example—just as it left the showroom—with only 69 miles on the odometer.

1975

XR-750

roduced in 1970, the XR-750 was
purpose-built racing bike aimed at
t-track competition. The engine
s based on that of the Sportster.
ts first two years of production,
e XR came with iron cylinders and
ads, which proved a weak link. Alloy
inders and heads were substituted
972, and performance improved
mendously. Maximum compres-

sion with iron components was 8.0:1;
the alloy parts allowed ratios as high
as 10.5:1, adding 20 horsepower. The
XR-750 had dual carbs and by 1975,
a high-mounted megaphone
exhaust. Though downsized to 750-
cc, from the Sportster's 1000-cc,
these engines produced a whopping
90 horsepower, all of which could be
set free with just a quarter-turn of the

throttle. To help rein in that power, the XR-750 gained a rear disc brake in 1972.

For more than a decade, the XR-750 tore up the dirt tracks, and even made its mark on some road-racing courses.

1977

XLCR SPORTSTER

Harley-Davidson joined the cafe-racer craze of the '70s with the uncharacteristic (for Harley-Davidson) XLCR. Penned by "Willie C." Davidson, the Sportster-based model came only in black with 7-spoke cast wheels, small handlebar fairing, "coffin-shaped" fuel tank, special 2-into-1-into-2 exhaust, rear-set footpegs prompting a "backwards" shift pedal, and a racing-style seat with tail fairing.

1977 XLCR SPORTSTER | 153

Thanks in part to the snake-like exhaust system, the XLCR's 1000-cc V-twin put out more power than the standard Sportster motor, making it one of the quickest street Harleys of the day.

The XLCRs were the only bikes built during the AMF years that didn't have "AMF" included in the tank logo; instead, it appeared as a small stick-on label affixed to the side cover. The intent was that owners could easily peel them off—and many did.

THOUGH A CLASSIC AMONG COLLECTORS TODAY, THE XLCR WASN'T WELL RECEIVED WHEN NEW, AND PRODUCTION LASTED ONLY TWO YEARS (1977 AND '78).

1978
FLHS ELECTRA-GLIDE

While the "FLH" nomenclature typically invokes the image of full-tilt, luggage laden touring bike, adding the "S" suffix in 1978 brought instead a stripped machine resembling the FLs of old. Adding to the illusion were simple block-lettered tank badges and a large headlight nacelle.

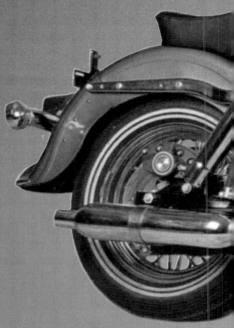

Everything seen on this example is factory equipment, including the twin-stripe whitewall tires and chrome battery cover, as it has never been modified or restored. It is an original bike that has essentially never been ridden.

An 80-cubic-inch motor was introduced for 1978, and eventually became standard on Big Twins. This bike, however, has the 74-cubic inch version, as the "1200" fender badges attest.

1978

FXS LOW RIDER

Unlike Harley-Davidson's other factory custom for 1977—the less than successful XLCR cafe racer—the FXS Low Rider proved an instant hit, quickly becoming the company's top seller.

With its low-set handlebars, cast spoke wheels, 2-into-1 header, and ground-hugging stance, this low-slung, dragster-like cruiser was more in tune with the typical Harley-rider's tastes.

A matte-black instrument panel topped the "Fat Bob" style fuel tank, which carried decals that echoed the typestyle of Harley's earliest bikes—with the AMF prefix added, of course.

BOTH KICK AND ELECTRIC STARTERS WERE SUPPLIED TO WAKE THE 74-CUBIC-INCH V-TWIN.

1978

XL-1000 SPORTSTER

Though Harley-Davidson's 75th anniversary took place while under the ownership of AMF, that certainly didn't prevent the release of special models to herald the occasion.

Sportsters haven't typically been chosen to carry such honors, but along with some specially trimmed Big Twins, Harley built a limited run of celebratory XL-1000s in 1978. Highlighting the jet-black paint were gold striping and gold-tinted cast wheels, while a saddle trimmed in genuine leather added a touch of class. Also on hand were a special 2-into-1 exhaust header and dual front disc brakes.

ALL SPORTSTERS THAT YEAR BOASTED A NEW ELECTRONIC IGNITION SYSTEM TO REPLACE THE OLD POINTS AND COIL SETUP.

1980

FXWG
WIDE GLIDE

Harley had introduced the idea
of the "factory custom" back
in 1971 with the FX Super Glide,
but went one step further when
it brought out the FXWG Wide
Glide in 1980.

This one truly had a chopper appearance, with a flamed Fat Bob fuel tank and wide-spaced fork tubes embracing a 21-inch spoked front wheel. A stepped saddle, forward-mounted brake and shift pedals, bucket style headlight, pull-back handlebars, and bobbed rear fender completed the look.

Powering the Wide Glide was Harley's 80-cubic-inch Big Twin—a fact

advertised by the "ham can" air cleaner that substituted for the oval air cleaner used on the 74-inch V-twin.

1981
HERITAGE EDITION

One of the first in what would become a series of retro designs, the 1981 Heritage Edition was fitted with a '60s-style headlight nacelle, twin chrome-covered rear shocks, classic Buddy Seat with handrail, and fringed seat and saddle bags. Only the front disc brake and "ham can" air cleaner betrayed its modern vintage. Power came from an 80-cubic-inch V-twin, a displacement that was revived in 1978 after having last been used on a '41 flathead.

ADDING TO THE NOSTALGIC LOOK WAS AN ODD OLIVE AND ORANGE PAINT SCHEME, WHICH MAY HAVE CARRIED SOME HISTORICAL SIGNIFICANCE BUT WASN'T VERY POPULAR WITH BUYERS, MEANING THE '81 HERITAGE IS A RARE SIGHT TODAY.

1981
FXB
STURGIS

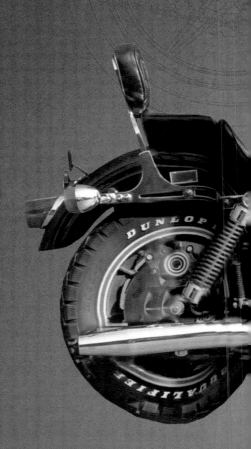

THE FXB STURGIS
TOOK ITS NAME FROM
THE WEEK-LONG
MOTORCYCLE EVENT HELD
EACH SUMMER IN
STURGIS, SOUTH DAKOTA.

The FX designation identified it as a version of the Low Rider, the B indicated that both primary (engine to transmission) and secondary (transmission to rear wheel) drive was via belt rather than conventional chain. Bathed in black, with only small touches of orange and chrome trim, the Sturgis proved to be a very popular model.

Harley-Davidson regained its independence in 1981 with a management buyback from AMF.

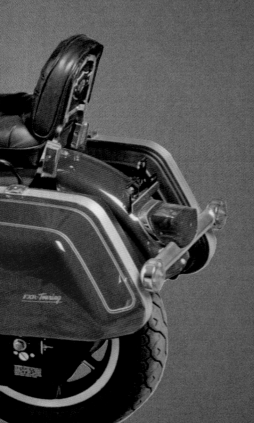

1984

FXRT

WHEN INTRODUCED IN 1982,
THE FXR WAS HERALDED AS A
LANDMARK MOTORCYCLE FOR
HARLEY-DAVIDSON.

A stiffer frame with Sportster-style forks provided better handling than any previous Big Twin, while rubber engine mounts and a five-speed transmission resulted in a smoother, quieter highway ride. The 1984 version was among the chosen few to get the new Evolution V2 motor, which further enhanced the FXRT's touring capabilities.

1984

XR-1000 SPORTSTER

Harley's XR-750 racing bike enjoyed such success on the nation's flat tracks that a street version was introduced in 1983 to capitalize on the notoriety. Though based on the stripped down XLX Sportster, the XR-1000 was fitted with heads similar to those found on the racing version.

These brought intake ports entering the rear of both cylinders fed by dual carburetors, and front exiting exhaust ports emptying into high-mounted dual mufflers.

The modifications resulted in a output of nearly 70 horsepower, a figure only dreamed of by other Sportsters, and gave the XR-1000 acceleration unequalled by any previous street motorcycle Harley had built.

Unfortunately, the race-bred hardware that made the XR-1000 quite fast also made it quite expensive. At nearly $2000 more than the XLX, not enough riders appreciated the difference, and the XR would fade into the sunset after the 1984 model run.

1986

XLH 1100

The Sportster motor introduced in 1957 enjoyed a long life, even by Harley-Davidson's standards. It wasn't until 1986 that it saw any significant changes, but those changes made quite a difference.

Adopting some of the same Evolution technology that had so improved Big Twins two years earlier, 1986 Sportsters got their own version of the Evolution powerplant that was smoother and more reliable than the old design. The new motor now came in two displacements: the original's 883-cc and a larger 1100-cc version. The latter was enlarged to 1200-cc for 1988.

1988

FXSTS

Springer forks made a comeback in 1988 after 37 years in hibernation.

Advancements in technology had increased their effectiveness, but the look mimicked those that were last used on WL 45-cubic-inch V-twins in 1951, and Big Twins in 1948.

CHOSEN TO SHOWCASE THE NEW FORKS WAS THE 1988 FXSTS.

The name said it all: "FX" indicated a Big Twin motor in a cruiser frame, "ST" stood for "Softail," Harley's innovative rear suspension that looked like a hardtail but provided far more cushioning; and "S" denoted the new springer forks, which adopted a forward-mounted shock absorber and were brightly plated in chrome.

Since 1988 marked Harley's 85th anniversary, a trio of bikes carried special graphics and badges to commemorate the occasion. The FXSTS was one of the chosen. Anniversary decals graced the front fender and fuel tank, while our featured model wears accessory cloisonné emblems atop the fuel-filler caps.

1990

FLSTF
FAT BOY

HARLEY-DAVIDSON HAS PRODUCED NUMEROUS SPECIALTY MACHINES OVER THE YEARS, BUT FEW HAVE HAD THE IMPACT OF THE FLSTF FAT BOY THAT DEBUTED IN 1990.

1990 FLSTF FAT BOY | 199

THE FAT BOY'S SIMPLE YET ELEGANT SILVER PAINT SCHEME WAS ENHANCED BY A MATCHING FRAME, WITH SUBTLE YELLOW HIGHLIGHTS BEING THE ONLY IDIOSYNCRASY IN THE MONOCHROMATIC THEME.

The Fat Boy was alone in its use of solid 16-inch wheels both front and rear, and got a slimmed-down skirted front fender to help differentiate it from other retro-styled Big Twins. It even got its own monogrammed air cleaner.

1991
FXDB STURGIS

Harley's first Sturgis model of 1980 was powered by a Shovelhead motor; the 1991 edition had the Evolution V-twin (introduced in 1984) nestled in a new Dynaglide chassis. But the theme remained the same, with touches of chrome highlighting acres of black paint with orange accents—Harley's corporate colors.

This Sturgis model celebrated the 50th anniversary of the Black Hills rally held each summer in Sturgis, South Dakota. And like its predecessor, the long, lean Sturgis is a collector's item today.

1992
FXDB
DAYTONA

Daytona Beach, Florida, and Sturgis,
South Dakota, both host a major
motorcycle event each year, and
both attract thousands of riders.

1992 FXDB DAYTONA | 207

PRODUCTION WAS LIMITED. ONLY 1700 DAYTONAS WERE BUILT, WHICH WAS NOT NEAR ENOUGH TO GO AROUND.

In 1991, Harley-Davidson celebrated the 50th anniversary of the Sturgis rally with a specially trimmed FXDB Sturgis model. The following year, a similar tribute was paid to the 50th anniversary of the Daytona meet with the FXDB Daytona.

While the Sturgis wore somber black highlighted with touches of orange, the Daytona was dressed in brighter shades with a more traditional level of chrome trim and boasted Harley's first true pearl paint job. On the tank was a special decal announcing the 50th anniversary as taking place in March of 1991.

Triple disc brakes were bolted to color-matched cast wheels, and highway pegs were mounted to the lower frame.

1993

FLSTN

AMONG THE MOST COLLECTIBLE OF MODERN HARLEYS IS THE 1993 FLSTN, AFFECTIONATELY KNOWN AS THE "COW GLIDE."

UNLIKE THE FX SPECIALS OF THE ERA, THE COW GLIDE CARRIED THE HEAVY FORK AND SKIRTED FENDERS OF THE FL MODELS.

And with its black-and-white paint, whitewall tires, and unique bovine trim (even the tank and saddlebags carried a hint of heifer), it's not difficult to understand why.

Built only in 1993, just 2700 copies were produced —far below the level of demand. The FLSTN was offered in different two-tone colors for the next several years, but those lucky enough to get one of the black-and-white '93s were rewarded with an instant classic and a sure-fire future collectible.

1993

FXDWG WIDE GLIDE

In what had become a customary gesture, Harley-Davidson celebrated its 90th anniversary in 1993 with a select group of specially trimmed models. One of those chosen to carry the honors was the FXDWG Wide Glide.

Making its debut in 1980, the Wide Glide got its name from its widely spaced fork tubes. Added to that were a 21-inch spoked front wheel, high pull-back handlebars, forward-mounted foot pegs, bobbed rear fender, and a Fat Bob fuel tank sprayed with flames. Those same features—this time on the new Dyna chassis—marked the '93 Wide Glide save for the flame paint job; in its place, the anniversary edition wore a suit of charcoal and sliver—with, of course, anniversary buttons.

1994

BUELL S2 THUNDERBOLT

After branching off to build his own motorcycles in the 1980s, former Harley-Davidson engineer Erik Buell came up with some innovative technologies that met with a roller-coaster of success.

1994 BUELL S2 THUNDERBOLT | 219

THE SPORTSTER-BASED ENGINE ENSURED THAT IT SOUNDED LIKE NO OTHER SPORTBIKE ON THE ROAD.

Although his first effort was a racing motorcycle, Buell began building street bikes in 1987, the first being a series of sportbikes powered by Harley-Davidson's Sportster-based, racing-inspired XR-1000 V-twin. The bikes were generally not as quick as those from Japanese and European rivals, but they handled very well, and the V-twin produced loads of low-end torque and a distinctive exhaust note.

In 1993, Harley-Davidson bought into Buell. By combining the latest hardware from Buell with the financial backing of Harley-Davidson, the S2 Thunderbolt was poised to make a full-scale attack on the popular sportbike market. The S2, boasting Buell's latest technical refinements, promised to be a stronger contender. Powering the S2 was a modified 1203-cc V-twin from the Harley-Davidson Sportster.

The combination of a low center of gravity, sophisticated suspension, and compact 55-inch wheelbase ensured that the Buell S2 Thunderbolt handled like no other Harley-powered bike before it.

1994

FLHTC ULTRA CLASSIC ELECTRA GLIDE

Despite its success with cruisers, Harley-Davidson maintained its presence in the touring market where the Hydra-Glide, Duo-Glide, and Electra Glide had made their marks.

Harley's top tourer for 1994 was the FLHTC Ultra Classic Electra Glide. Fully dressed, it wore a plush two-place saddle, electronic cruise control, cavernous saddlebags and trunk, and a full fairing playing host to an AM/FM/cassette stereo and CB radio—just the ticket for the rider who wanted to heed the call of the wild without forfeiting the comforts of home.

1995

FXSTSB
BAD BOY

A NEW ADDITION TO HARLEY'S CRUISER LINE FOR 1995 WAS THE FXSTSB BAD BOY.

Though based on the existing Softail Springer, Bad Boys were cloaked in black from their '40s-style springer fork to their bobbed rear fender, with striping in red, blue, or yellow. Decorating the tank was a jeweled metal badge unique to the Bad Boy. Chrome trim was used sparingly but effectively. Both the slotted rear wheel and spoked front wheel were fitted with drilled brake discs.

The Bad Boy returned for '96 and '97 after which it was discontinued, ensuring its status as a modern collectible.

1998

FLHRCI
ROAD KING

Harley-Davidson offered three versions of
the Road King for 1998. The standard FLHR
could be powered by a carbureted or
fuel-injected V-twin, while the Classic came
standard with fuel injection.

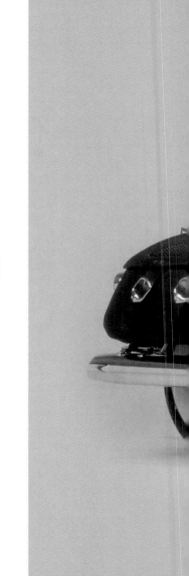

1998 FLHRCI ROAD KING | 231

An assortment of three-dimensional badges set the Classic apart from the base Road King, and the hard leather-covered saddlebags were another visual clue. The wide whitewall tires and slanted exhaust tips continued the division between the two versions of the popular open-road machine. Our featured bike wears Harley's 95th anniversary paint scheme and emblems.

1998
FLHTCUI

BY COMBINING ALL THE COMFORTS
OF HOME WITH A FULL COMPLEMENT
OF ELECTRONICS, HARLEY CREATED THE
ULTIMATE TOURING RIG.

THE FLHTCUI WAS THE BEST-EQUIPPED HARLEY EVER OFFERED, LEAVING LITTLE TO BE DESIRED.

In back was a trio of hard luggage capable of swallowing copious quantities of travel gear. Both the rider and passenger were coddled in thickly padded, form-fitting thrones that provided more than adequate comfort on long trips. Not only did the enormous fairing protect the riders from the elements, it housed a host of electronic conveniences.

1998 FLHTCUI | 237

1998

FLSTS
HERITAGE
SPRINGER

1998 FLSTS HERITAGE SPRINGER | **239**

THE HERITAGE SPRINGER, INTRODUCED IN 1997, RETURNED FOR 1998 UNALTERED IN MECHANICAL SPECIFACTIONS.

But while the '97 versions came only in white, the '98s were dressed in black. Once again, striping was red or blue, and a '40s-style emblem graced the tank.

From the Springer forks to the wide whitewalls to the fringed saddlebags, the "Old Boy," as it was nicknamed, boasted styling reminiscent of a '40s-vintage bike. The example photographed carries some optional accessories, such as teardrop front-axle flares.

1998

FLTRI ROAD GLIDE

NEW FOR 1998, THE ROAD GLIDE HARKENED BACK TO THE FLT OF THE 1980S.

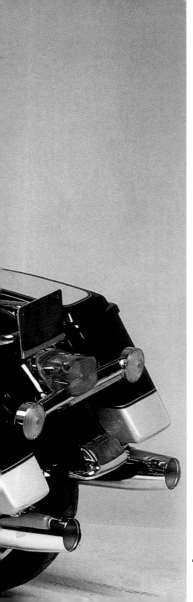

The Road Glide was easily differentiated by its half fairing fitted with dual headlamps. Like Harley's other touring models, the speedometer and tachometer resided in a fairing-mounted instrument panel instead of atop the fuel tank. Also included were an AM/FM stereo cassette, voltmeter, oil-pressure gauge, clock, and fuel gauge. Buyers had a choice of feeding the 80-cubic-inch V-twin through a carburetor or fuel-injection unit, the latter was an option that delivered almost 10 percent more torque.

1998

FXDWG
WIDE
GLIDE

1998 FXDWG WIDE GLIDE | **247**

FIRST INTRODUCED IN 1980, THE WIDE GLIDE REMAINED A POPULAR MODEL IN THE BIG TWIN LINE.

As in its predecessor, the tall 21-inch spoked front wheel rolled between the namesake wide-set, raked-back forks. Forward foot controls lent a long, lean look to the chassis, and combined with the "ape hanger" handlebars, gave the rider a natural laid-back posture. A deeply stepped saddle provided ample comfort for both the rider and passenger, a welcome feature since the 5.2-gallon Fat Bob tank carried the Wide Glide a long way between fuel stops. This example wears the winged tank emblem and Midnight Red and Champaign Pearl paint of the 95th anniversary models.

1998

XL-1200C
SPORTSTER

1998 XL-1200C SPORTSTER | 251

All XL-1200 Customs for 1998 featured a 16-inch slotted wheel in black with a 21-inch spoked wheel up front. Handlebars mounted on risers hovered over a lone speedometer and the bullet-style headlight shunned the "eyebrow" warning light panel found on other Sportsters.

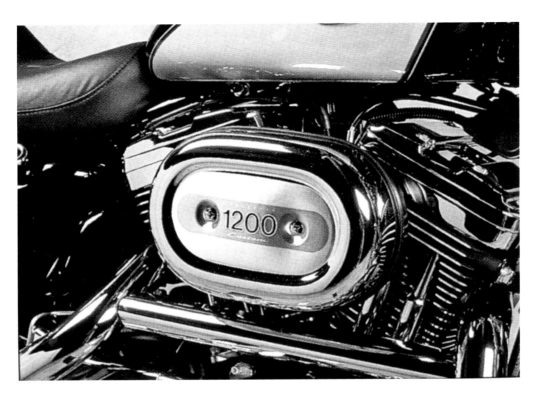

Mechanically identical to the standard XL-1200C, the 95th anniversary edition wore the special cloisonné tank badges and Midnight Red and Champagne Pearl paint scheme reserved exclusively for anniversary models.

OUR FEATURED EXAMPLE ADDS A PERSONAL TOUCH WITH A SELECTION OF HARLEY-DAVIDSON ACCESSORIES.

2000

FXSTD
DEUCE

THE COMBINATION OF CUSTOM APPEARANCE AND CONTEMPORARY FEATURES MADE THE DEUCE A HIGHLY DESIRABLE CREATION.

FROM THE FIRST DAY OF THE DEUCE'S INTRODUCTION FOR MODEL-YEAR 2000, HARLEY-DAVIDSON HAD A TOUGH TIME KEEPING UP WITH DEMAND.

Two of the Deuce's strongest visual cues were the stretched fuel tank and the straight-cut rear fender. Perhaps not as obvious were the unique "turbine blade" solid rear wheel, graceful tapered fork legs, and small teardrop headlight. Sitting atop the fuel tank was a full-length chrome console housing the traditional lone speedometer, while curved chrome risers brought the cushioned grips closer to the riders' eager hands.

2002

FXSTB
NIGHT
TRAIN

WHEN INTRODUCED FOR 1999, THE
NIGHT TRAIN WAS A STUDY IN BASIC BLACK.

And though the Night Train had undergone some subtle changes in the intervening years, the look remained true to its sinister origins.

The following year, Jade Sunglo Pearl was added as a color choice. But all Night Trains shared the crinkle-black trim that set this model apart: The engine and transmission were both cloaked in black, as were traditionally chromed items such as the oil tank, air-filter cover, rear-fender braces, and tank-mounted instrument panel. Yet a few trim pieces remained bright— just enough to be able to spot a Night Train in the dark.

THE FIRST NIGHT TRAINS WERE POWERED BY AN 80-CUBIC-INCH EVOLUTION V-TWIN, WHICH GAVE WAY TO THE TWIN CAM 88B FOR 2000.

2002

VRSCA V-ROD

Although Harley-Davidson's traditional bikes shared a number of key characteristics, including V-twin engines featuring a 45-degree-angle V, air cooling, and two-valve cylinder heads, none of that mattered when the V-twin Racing Street Custom (VRSC), or just V-Rod, was rolled out for the 2002 model year.

2002 VRSCA V-ROD | 269

In the mid-Nineties, Harley-Davidson campaigned the VR1000, a racing bike powered by a liquid-cooled 60-degree V-twin that featured double-overhead cam, four-valve cylinder heads—basically the same engine found on the V-Rod.

EVEN THOUGH THE V-ROD ENGINE WAS UNLIKE ANY RETAIL HARLEY-DAVIDSON POWERPLANT BEFORE IT, IT WASN'T NEW TO HARLEY ITSELF.

THE HIGH-TECH V-ROD "REVOLUTION V-TWIN" ENGINE DISPLACED 1131 CUBIC CENTIMETERS.

Though of modest displacement by company standards, the Revolution engine's 115-horsepower output bested that of any other retail Harley mill before it.

The Revolution engine was not the V-Rod's only departure from Harley-Davidson canon. Longer and lower than other Harley bikes, the V-Rod featured an exposed tube frame, aluminum body panels, an oval headlamp, and an especially steep fork angle. Predictably, many Harley-Davidson traditionalists took issue with the radical V-Rod. However, the bike's power and design have made it a classic in its own right.

2003

FXSTD ANNIVERSARY MODEL

IN 2003, HARLEY-DAVIDSON
CELEBRATED 100 YEARS OF PRODUCTION.
FROM HUMBLE BEGINNINGS IN A BACKYARD
SHED BEHIND THE DAVIDSON HOME,

2003 FXSTD ANNIVERSARY MODEL | 275

Harley-Davidson grew to be one of the best-known motorcycle brands in the world with a fanatical following. In late August of 2003, more than 250,000 fans came to the Harley-Davidson 100th Anniversary Celebration and Party in Milwaukee. The 2003 model-year Harleys had special anniversary badges. Otherwise, changes were minor that year with the FXSTD Softail Deuce

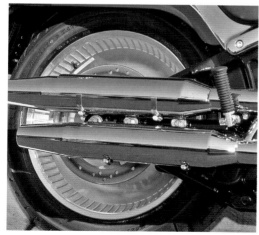

gaining a wider 160-series rear tire. There was more to the Deuce than its "custom bike" look. The Twin Cam 88B motor provided strong performance and the softail frame contributed to good handling and a comfortable ride.

2006

FLHTCUSE

AS HARLEY'S MILE-EATER, THE ELECTRA GLIDE CLASSIC ULTRA WAS BIG AND PACKED WITH CONVENIENCES.

The standard radio was an Advanced Audio System by Harman Kardon with AM/FM/WB/CD. XM satellite radio, hands-free cell-phone module, and CB bike-to-bike communications and intercom were optional. Also available were factory Screamin' Eagle performance upgrades.

The "Screamin' Eagle l03" on this bike signified that the 88-cubic-inch motor was bored and stroked to l03 cid and included other performance modifications.

The Screamin' Eagle's extra power could restore some of the performance lost through the weight of two passengers and their gear.

NEW FOR 2006 WAS AN UPGRADED CHARGING SYSTEM TO COPE WITH ADDED ELECTRICAL EQUIPMENT AND A REDESIGNED CLUTCH LINKAGE THAT REDUCED EFFORT SIGNIFICANTLY.

There was also adjustable rear air suspension to cope with heavy loads. By 2006, fuel injection was standard on Electra Glide Classic Ultras.

2009

BUELL
1125CR

BUELL, HARLEY-DAVIDSON'S
PERFORMANCE SPORTBIKE
SUBSIDIARY, WAS FULLY OWNED
BY THE COMPANY BY 2003.

In 2007, Buell moved away from using Harley Sportster engines, choosing instead a much more advanced double-overhead-cam, 4-valve-per-cylinder, water-cooled, 72-degree, 1125-cc V-twin built by Rotax of Austria.

Reported to produce 146 horse-power—far more than the Sport-ster-based engines—the Rotax went into a model called the 1125R, essentially a sportbike without a full fairing.

THE 1125R TURNED OUT TO BE THE FINAL PRODUCTION BUELLS BUILT UNDER THE HARLEY-DAVIDSON UMBRELLA.

A variation of this bike arrived for 2009 as the 1125CR, the "CR" signifying its "Café Racer" styling. Although more than 130,000 Buells had been sold over the years, profits were not always impressive, and the parent company decided to concentrate its efforts on its traditional cruiser and touring bikes.

2013

FLHX

THE FLHX STREET GLIDE WAS A STRIPPED-DOWN VERSION OF THE ELECTRA GLIDE TOURING BIKE WITH A LOWER, SPORTIER LOOK.

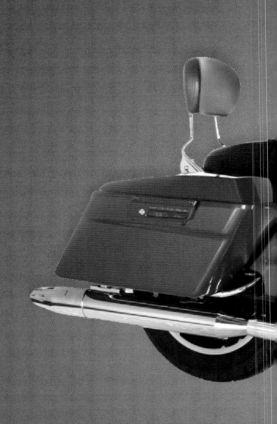

The Street Glide had hard saddle bags, rear air suspension, and many other touring bike comforts, but it didn't look like a rolling Barcalounger. The Street Glide was introduced in 2006, and in 2007 its standard engine size was increased from 88 cid to 96 cid. For 2011, the engine grew to 103 cid and horsepower was estimated to be about 85.

The 103 engine was paired with a new six-speed transmission that replaced the previous five-speed. An important safety upgrade for 2008 was the switch to Brembo brakes with a newly optional antilock system.

2017

CVO
PRO
STREET
BREAKOUT

IN "THE OLD DAYS," IF YOU WANTED YOUR MOTORCYCLE TO STAND OUT, YOU HAD TO DO THE CUSTOMIZING YOURSELF.

But what if you could just buy a customized bike right off the showroom floor? Harley-Davidson has been selling custom-look bikes since 1999, The motor company's Custom Vehicle Operations (CVO) has produced a variety of limited-edition machines, typically picking just two to four models each year to get special treatment.

2017 CVO PRO STREET BREAKOUT | 301

ARGUABLY THE MOST STUNNING OF THE 2017 CVO CROP WAS THE CVO PRO STREET BREAKOUT.

Riding the company's softail frame (which looks like the hardtail frames of yore, but has a separate rear section that pivots over bumps), it combined unique paint, wheels, bodywork, and steeply raked inverted forks with Harley-Davidson's 110-cubic-inch Twin Cam 110B engine to create a bike that screamed "custom" with a very strong V-twin voice. And its few lucky buyers didn't have to waste their weekends creating it.

A unique paint treatment, distinctive headlight fairing, lower-frame chin spoiler, and Screamin' Eagle air intake helped give the Pro Street Breakout a custom look, despite the fact it came that way right from the factory.

2018

FAT BOB

THE FAT BOB NAME FIRST APPEARED IN 2008 IN HARLEY'S DYNA RANGE, BUT IT MOVED TO THE SOFTAIL LINE FOR 2018.

The Softail hides the rear suspension so the bike has the style of a vintage bike with no rear suspension. That suspension was updated and the frame was considerably more rigid for better ride and handling.

Braking was also improved with dual front rotors and four-piston calipers. An antilock system was optional. Harley introduced a new Milwaukee-Eight line of engines for 2017. True to Harley tradition, the valves were operated by pushrods, but there were now four valves per cylinder in the V-twin motor or "eight" in total. The Milwaukee-Eight came in 107-cid and 114-cid displacements. Harley claimed the new engines produced more power, yet with less heat and vibration.

The styling was a departure for Harley-Davidson with matte-finished paint and flat-black trim instead of the usual glossy paint with liberal use of chrome trim.

The oval LED headlight was another break from Harley tradition.

2018 FAT BOB | 311

2019
FXDR

2019 FXDR | 313

Harley-Davidson shocked traditionalists with the announcement of the LiveWire electric motorcycle, due to go on sale in late 2019. Future plans also called for a new sportbike, a middle-weight platform, and an on-road/off-road adventure touring bike as part of the company's "More Roads to Harley-Davidson" growth strategy. However, the new game plan didn't mean that Harley-Davidson was neglecting its core touring and cruiser bikes.

A case in point was the new-for-2019 FXDR 114 cruiser. The standard engine was a Milwaukee-Eight 114 with 119 lb-ft of torque and an estimated 90 horsepower. As the name implied, the big V-twin had a 114 cubic inches of displacement or 1868-cc.

HARLEY DESCRIBED THE FXDR AS "LIKE A DRAG RACER CROSSED WITH A FIGHTER JET."

2019 FXDR | 317

BUT THE FXDR WAS MORE THAN LOOKS AND POWER.

Harley used more lightweight aluminum in the FXDR, including an alloy rear swingarm that reduced unsprung weight. The result was better handling than expected from a big cruiser. Perhaps that was another way to lead more buyers to Harley-Davidson.